Book is dedicated to the people who created personal experience for me and different jobs on which i learnt alot.

CHAPTER 1

importance of Business communication

Business communication is critical for the success of any organization. It allows for the effective exchange of ideas and information, enables collaboration and coordination among employees, and helps to build and maintain relationships with customers and other stakeholders.

Effective business communication is essential for building trust and fostering positive relationships with customers, employees, and other stakeholders. Clear and timely communication can help to prevent misunderstandings and conflicts, and can also facilitate problem-solving and decision-making.

In addition, effective business communication is essential for coordinating the efforts of employees and teams. It allows managers to delegate tasks, provide feedback, and monitor progress, which helps to ensure that projects and initiatives are completed on time and to the desired level of quality.

Effective business communication also helps to build a positive corporate culture and can contribute to the overall success of an organization. Clear and open communication can help to build trust and foster a sense of community among employees, which can lead to increased job satisfaction and motivation, and ultimately, higher productivity and performance.

In today's fast-paced business environment, it is also important for organizations to have effective communication channels in place to respond quickly to changes in the market and to stay competitive. This includes being able to communicate effectively with customers through social media and other digital channels, as well as being able to quickly share information and updates with employees and stakeholders.

In conclusion, effective business communication is essential for the success of any organization. It enables the efficient exchange of ideas and information, helps to build and maintain relationships, and is critical for coordinating the efforts of employees and teams. In today's fast-paced business environment, it is also important for organizations to have effective communication channels in place to respond quickly to changes in the market and stay competitive.

Lets understand the communication with the help of small yet powerful story.

Once upon a time, in a bustling city, there was a small business called "Efficient Communications." The company specialized in helping other businesses improve their communication strategies and processes.

The owner and founder, Sarah, had always been passionate about the power of effective communication. She believed that clear and concise communication was essential for any business to succeed. With her background in marketing and her natural talent for connecting with people, she decided to start her own company to help others achieve the same level of success.

Efficient Communications quickly became known as the go-to company for businesses looking to improve their internal and external communication. Sarah and her team worked tirelessly to understand each client's unique needs and tailor their services accordingly.

One of their most successful projects was with a large retail chain. The company was struggling with poor communication among its employees, which was leading to confusion and mistakes on the sales floor. Efficient Communications stepped in and implemented a comprehensive training program for all employees, focused on clear and effective communication.

The results were astounding. Within just a few months, the retail chain saw a significant increase in sales and customer satisfaction. The employees were able to communicate more effectively with each other and with customers, leading to a smoother shopping experience for everyone.

Word of the retail chain's success quickly spread, and Efficient Communications' reputation as a leading expert in business communication continued to grow. They worked with a variety of other clients, from small startups to large corporations, and helped them all improve their communication strategies and processes.

Sarah was thrilled with the success of her company and the positive impact it was having on the business community. She knew that effective communication was the key to success for any business, and she was proud to be helping others achieve that success.

As Efficient Communications continued to thrive, Sarah decided to expand the company's services to include other areas of business, such as branding, marketing and customer service. With a strong foundation in communication and a dedicated team of experts, Efficient Communications became a one-stop shop for businesses looking to improve all aspects of their operations.

Years passed and Efficient Communications had become a household name. Businesses from all over the world reached out to the company for help, and Sarah and her team were always more than happy to oblige. They had helped thousands of businesses improve their communication and overall operations, and their success was a testament to the power of effective communication.

Efficient Communications had not only helped other businesses succeed but also became one of the most successful companies in its industry. Sarah's passion for communication had led to the creation of a company that had a positive impact on the business world and helped others to achieve their goals. The moral of the story is that good communication is the key to success in any business and Efficient Communications was a shining example of this.

CHAPTER 2

business without business communication

A business without effective communication would struggle to survive. Communication is the backbone of any organization, and without it, operations would grind to a halt, relationships would break down, and productivity would plummet.

Without effective communication, employees would be unable to understand their roles and responsibilities, and managers would be unable to delegate tasks or provide feedback. This would lead to confusion, misunderstandings, and mistakes, which would ultimately result in poor quality work and delayed projects.

Without communication, there would be no way for employees to collaborate and share ideas. Innovation and creativity would be stifled, and the organization would struggle to adapt to changes in the market or to identify new opportunities.

In the absence of effective communication, it would also be impossible to build and maintain positive relationships with customers, suppliers, and other stakeholders. Customers would be left in the dark about the status of their orders or the progress of their projects, and suppliers would be unable to coordinate deliveries or resolve issues.

Effective communication is also essential for building a positive corporate culture and for fostering a sense of community among employees. Without communication, employees would be isolated and disconnected, and morale and motivation would suffer.

In today's fast-paced business environment, effective communication is also critical for staying competitive. Organizations that are unable to communicate effectively with customers through social media and other digital channels would struggle to keep up with the competition and would be at a disadvantage in the market.

In conclusion, a business without effective communication would be unable to function properly. It would struggle to coordinate the efforts of employees and teams, to build and maintain relationships with customers and other stakeholders, and to stay competitive in the market. Effective communication is essential for the success of any organization, and without it, the organization would struggle to survive.

Let's understand this point with the different small and powerful story.

Once upon a time, in a bustling city, there was a small business called "Silent Solutions." The company specialized in providing a wide range of services to other businesses, but with one major problem: they had no proper communication strategy in place.

The owner and founder, John, had always been more focused on making money and expanding his business, rather than investing in communication infrastructure. He believed that as long as the work was getting done, there was no need to spend time and resources on communication.

Silent Solutions quickly became known for their low prices and efficient service, but it wasn't long before their lack of communication started to catch up with them. Clients were often confused and frustrated by the lack of clear instructions and updates on their projects. Employees were left in the dark about important decisions and often found themselves working on tasks that were no longer relevant.

One of their most significant projects was with a large manufacturing company. The manufacturing company was looking for a cost-effective solution to streamline their production process. Silent Solutions stepped in and provided them with a new production line, but with no proper communication, the installation process was chaotic and the production line was not able to operate efficiently. The manufacturing company was extremely dissatisfied with the outcome and decided to terminate the contract with Silent Solutions.

The negative feedback from the manufacturing company spread quickly, and Silent Solutions' reputation as a reliable and professional service provider was damaged. They struggled to attract new clients and retain their existing ones, as their lack of communication was causing delays, mistakes and misunderstandings.

John was shocked by the rapid decline of his business, but he was not willing to admit that the lack of communication was the problem. He tried to blame the employees and the clients, but the truth was that the root of the problem was the company's communication infrastructure.

Years passed and Silent Solutions was barely surviving. John had to lay off employees and cut costs to keep the company afloat, but it was too little too late. Businesses from all over the city avoided Silent Solutions, and the company was on the brink of bankruptcy.

In the end, Silent Solutions had failed to understand the importance of communication in business. John's focus on making money had blinded him to the fact that good communication is essential for any business to succeed. His lack of investment in communication infrastructure had led to the downfall of his company, and it was a harsh lesson for the business community.

The moral of the story is that neglecting the importance of communication in business can lead to disastrous consequences, and it's essential to invest in proper communication infrastructure and strategies to ensure the success of any business.

JOHNY EINSTEIN

CHAPTER 3

*Is it Worthy to be
Courteous in Business?*

The value of courtesy in business cannot be overstated. It is a key component of effective communication and is essential for building and maintaining positive relationships with customers, employees, and other stakeholders.

When employees are courteous, they are able to create a positive and welcoming environment for customers. This is important because customers are more likely to return to a business where they feel valued and respected. Additionally, courteous employees can defuse difficult situations and turn unhappy customers into satisfied ones. By being polite and respectful, employees can also help to build trust and establish long-term customer relationships.

Courtesy also applies to internal communication and relationship building. When employees are courteous to one another, they create a positive and productive work environment. They are more likely to collaborate, share ideas, and provide support when needed. This can lead to increased productivity and improved job satisfaction.

when employees are courteous to their managers and supervisors, they are more likely to receive constructive feedback and guidance. This can help them to grow and develop professionally, which can benefit the organization as a whole.

Courtesy pays in dollars and cents, but its value greatly exceeds financial reward. We are now speaking of civility as an outgrowth of character, and good will is to a company as honor is to an individual. As long as he maintains his honor, he has something to work upon. In the same way, a business can lose all of its material assets and replace them with insurance money or something else, but if it loses its good will, it will discover in ninety out of one hundred instances that it is gone forever and that the business has become so weakened the only option is to completely restructure it and flush out the old institution.

In today's business environment, courtesy also plays an important role in online communication. As more and more business is conducted online, it is crucial to be courteous in email and social media interactions. This includes using proper grammar and spelling, avoiding slang or text-speak, and being professional at all times.

Ultimately, the value of courtesy in business is that it helps to create a positive and productive environment where people want to do business. It helps to build trust, establish long-term relationships, and defuse difficult situations. It also plays an important role in internal communication and relationship building among employees and managers.

courtesy is an essential part of effective communication and is crucial for building and maintaining positive relationships with customers, employees, and other stakeholders. It creates a positive and welcoming environment, helps to build trust and establish long-term relationships, and plays an important role in internal communication and relationship building. In today's business environment, it's also important to be courteous in online communication. Organizations that prioritize courtesy and encourage it among their employees will be more likely to succeed in the long run.

Discourtesy is one of the most powerful weapons in the arsenal of those who seek to destroy something, and business is no exception. It is far simpler to destroy something than it is to construct something new. One curt letter, one curt answer, or one impolite comment over the phone can sever a connection that has been cultivated over the course of many years. Even collection letters, regardless of how far past due the accounts are, bring in a greater amount of money when they are written diplomatically and with tact as opposed to when these two traits are left out of the letter. If you insult a man who owes you money, he will feel that the only way he can get even with you is by not paying you, and in most situations, he will be able to justify not paying you.

It's crucial that the men in charge inside the organization treat the people they oversee with respect. Companies reach a dead end when their leaders stop listening to and relying on their employees. However, it is rarely the seasoned commercial professional who creates the greatest trouble with his poor manners; rather, it is the greenhorn. Too many young men, especially those who have been lucky enough to secure worldly advantages, view the world as if it were an accident put here for their personal delight. It doesn't take long for them to get over this illusion in the corporate world, but occasionally they do a lot of damage in the meantime. Because nobody like interacting with someone who has a cocky, know-it-all attitude and the inefficiency that is nearly inseparable from a complete lack of expertise.

Every young man with any sense thinks he can change the world, but every old person who has experienced the world as it is realizes that this is impossible. About halfway through, they reach an agreement: "We'll keep working at it just the same." From there, business continues to improve. Tolerance, patience, and endless politeness are required on both sides if a compromise is to be reached.

BEFORE STARTING BUSINESS & JOB

CHAPTER 4

Role of Courtesy in the Business

Once upon a time, in a small village, there lived a kind and courteous young man named Jack. He was known throughout the village for his polite and respectful behavior towards others. He always greeted people with a warm smile and a friendly "hello," and he always made sure to use polite phrases such as "please" and "thank you."

One day, the village was visited by a group of travelers, who were looking for a place to rest for the night. Jack was the first person they met, and they were struck by his courteous behavior. He welcomed them to the village and offered to show them around and help them find a place to stay.

The travelers were impressed by Jack's kindness and

hospitality. He showed them the best places to eat and sleep in the village, and he even went out of his way to introduce them to some of the local residents.

As the travelers were leaving the village the next day, they thanked Jack for his hospitality. They told him that they had never met anyone as courteous and kind as him, and they wished that more people in the world were like him.

Jack was happy to have made a positive impression on the travelers and even happier that he was able to practice the courtesy. From that day on, he made an even greater effort to be courteous and kind to everyone he met. He believed that a little bit of kindness and courtesy can go a long way in making the world a better place.

As Jack grew older, he became known as the most courteous person in the village, and his reputation spread to the neighboring towns and cities. People from all over the region would come to the village just to meet him and learn from his example.

Years passed, and Jack's courteous behavior had a profound impact on the village. It became a more welcoming and friendly place, where people treated each other with kindness and respect. The village's economy thrived, and it became a popular tourist destination.

In the end, Jack's courteous behavior had made a significant difference in the lives of those around him, and his legacy lived on long after he passed away. The moral of the story is that a small act of courtesy can have a big impact on the world, and it's essential to always strive to be courteous and kind to others.

Same fact applies when it comes to business .

Putting courtesy into business is essential for creating positive relationships with customers and building a successful company. Here are some ways to incorporate courtesy into your business:

CHAPTER 5

Character Role in Business

What is character or personality?
A person's character or personality refers to the set of mental and emotional characteristics that defines an individual's nature. It encompasses a wide range of traits and behaviors that shape how a person interacts with the world around them. Some of the most common traits that make up a person's character or personality include:

Personality is often described as the set of traits that make people unique. These traits are usually measurable and consistent over time. Some theories suggest that personality is made up of five broad dimensions: extraversion, agreeableness, conscientiousness, neuroticism, and openness to experience.

Some people may have a more outgoing and sociable personality, while others may be more reserved and introverted. Some may be more easy-going and cooperative, while others may be more assertive and independent.

These traits can vary among individuals and change over time. Some people may have a more fixed or stable personality that does not change much, while others may have a more flexible or malleable personality that adapts to different situations.

Why Character Play Important Role In Business?

Character Plays An Important Role In Business Because It Directly Affects An Individual's Behavior And Decision-Making. It Shapes How A Person

Interacts With Colleagues, Clients, And Customers, And It Can Have A Significant Impact On The Overall Success Of A Business. Some Of The Ways In Which Character Can Play An Important Role In Business Include:

IN SUMMARY, CHARACTER PLAYS AN IMPORTANT ROLE IN BUSINESS BECAUSE IT HELPS INDIVIDUALS TO BUILD TRUST, MAKE ETHICAL DECISIONS, MANAGE CONFLICTS, AND INSPIRE OTHERS. IT CAN ALSO HAVE A SIGNIFICANT IMPACT ON THE OVERALL REPUTATION OF A BUSINESS AND ITS ABILITY TO ATTRACT NEW CLIENTS AND CUSTOMERS.

How People Develop The Character?

It is not the one day or few week task to complete aspirants develops it over a period of time and require the certain ingredients to make a solid character which speaks about you actually before you start speaking.

Ingredients of strong character or personality

The ingredients of a strong character or personality can vary depending on the individual and the specific traits and behaviors that are considered important. However, some common ingredients that are often associated with a strong character or personality include:

These ingredients may not be present in all individuals, but a person with a strong character or personality may possess a good number of them. It's important to note that these traits and behaviors are not fixed, and they can be developed and strengthened over time through effort and practice.

Once upon a time, there was a young man named Michael who had always dreamed of starting his own business. He was determined to succeed, but he knew that it would take more than just hard work and determination. He knew that a powerful character was essential for success in business.

Michael spent years studying the traits and behaviors of successful business leaders. He learned about the importance of honesty, integrity, and transparency in building trust with clients and customers. He studied the importance of empathy and self-control in making ethical decisions and managing conflicts. And he learned about the power of confidence and leadership in inspiring and motivating others.

With his newfound knowledge, Michael set out to build a powerful character of his own. He made a conscious effort to be honest and transparent in all of his interactions with others. He worked on developing his empathy and self-control, so that he could make ethical decisions and manage conflicts effectively. And he worked on building his confidence and leadership skills, so that he could inspire and motivate others.

Years passed, and Michael's hard work paid off. He was able to start his own business and quickly made a name for himself in the industry. His honesty, integrity, and transparency helped him to build trust with clients and customers, and his empathy and self-control helped him to make ethical decisions and manage conflicts effectively. His confidence and leadership skills inspired and motivated his employees, and they helped to create a positive and productive work environment.

Michael's business quickly became one of the most successful in the industry. His reputation as a leader with a powerful character spread far and wide, and he became an inspiration to others. He showed that with hard work, determination, and a powerful character, anyone can achieve success in business.

As Michael's business continued to thrive, he never forgot the importance of character. He continued to work on building his own character, and he also mentored other young entrepreneurs, teaching them the importance of developing a powerful character for success in business. He had learned that character is essential for anyone who wants to achieve success in the business world.

In the end, Michael's powerful character had played a vital role in his success. He had shown that with strong character traits, one can achieve success in business and also inspire others to do the same. The moral of the story is that a powerful character is essential for success in business, and it's important to continuously work on developing it.

> *I am pretty sure this story will help you a lot to become a lovely character in your life and business atmosphere. Always remember A lovely character is not only about the absence of negative traits, but it is also about the presence of positive qualities. People with a lovely character tend to be well-liked and respected, as they create a positive and uplifting atmosphere around them. They are easy to be around, and they make people feel good. It's important to note that having a lovely character does not mean that a person is perfect,*

everyone has their own flaws, but having a lovely character means that a person is trying to improve themselves and be a positive influence on others.

CHAPTER 6

*Dinning Manner
Matters A lot*

As we all aware of the fact that 21st century brought the lots of changes not only around the world but in our daily lifestyle as well including the dinning manners or table etiquettes least standard manners are expected from every one as we are going very much global especially when its common to meet people from different parts of the world.

Once upon a time, there was a young prince named George who had never learned proper table manners. He was used to eating with his hands and slurping his soup. His parents, the King and Queen, were worried that he would never learn the proper etiquette to be a successful ruler.

So, they hired a famous etiquette expert, Madame LaFleur, to teach the prince how to behave at the dinner table. The first lesson was on how to use utensils properly. The prince struggled at first, but with Madame LaFleur's patient guidance, he soon mastered the art of using a fork and knife.

The next lesson was on how to properly sip soup without slurping. The prince tried his best, but every time he picked up the spoon, he couldn't help but slurp loudly. Madame LaFleur tried different techniques to break the prince of his slurping habit, but nothing seemed to work.

Finally, in a moment of inspiration, Madame LaFleur suggested that the prince try eating his soup with a straw instead of a spoon. The prince was skeptical, but he was willing to try anything. To his surprise, he was able to sip his soup without a single slurp.

The prince was thrilled with his newfound success and couldn't wait to show off his new table manners to his parents. The King and Queen were impressed with their son's progress and were relieved that he would be able to conduct himself properly at state dinners and other royal events.

From that day on, the prince never slurped his soup again and was known as the most well-mannered prince in the land. Madame LaFleur was hailed as a genius and was offered a permanent position as the royal etiquette expert. The moral of the story is that sometimes; a little creativity can go a long way in learning proper table manners.

Table manners are important in business because they can have a significant impact on how a person is perceived by others. In a business, table manners can affect how colleagues, clients, and customers view an individual's professionalism, confidence, and attention to detail.

table manners play an important role in business, they can help to establish an individual as professional, confident and someone who pays attention to detail. They also provide an opportunity to build strong relationships with clients and colleagues. It's important to take the time to learn and practice good table manners in a business setting.

Key Manners At The Dining Table

There are several bad habits that should be avoided at the dining table in order to maintain good manners and etiquette. Some of these include:

It often common to have a dinner with clients , customer or colleagues in the restaurant or in the office canteen there are world class dinning habits in business which one must follow to show everlasting impression on the other person and they are called as world class dinning habits.

World-class dining habits in a business setting involve adhering to proper etiquette and manners in order to create a pleasant and professional atmosphere. Some examples of world-class dining habits include:

By following these world-class dining habits, individuals can create a pleasant and professional atmosphere at a business meal, and show respect for their colleagues, clients, and host. It can help to establish trust and positive relationship.

CHAPTER-7

*Telephone
Manners in Business*

Telephone or Mobile these devices are important part of our life like oxygen every day we speak over them even after that do we need to learn how to talk over them.? The answer is yes because every business start with the help of them and finished or remained uncompleted due to our absence or lack of telephone manners.

Telephone manners are an essential aspect of effective communication in a business setting. They play a crucial role in creating a positive impression and building strong relationships with customers, clients, and colleagues.

When it comes to creating a wonderful impression, the first thing to consider is the tone of voice. A warm and friendly tone can make the person on the other end of the line feel welcomed and valued. It can also indicate that the person on the other end is genuinely interested in helping them. On the other hand, a cold or indifferent tone can create an impression of disinterest or rudeness. Therefore, it's important to be aware of one's tone of voice and to make an effort to sound pleasant and approachable.

Another important aspect of telephone manners is the use of proper language and grammar. Speaking clearly and using proper grammar can help to convey professionalism and competence. It can also make it easier for the person on the other end of the line to understand what is being said and to respond appropriately. Using slang or informal language can create an impression of unprofessionalism and lack of expertise.

Additionally, it's important to be polite and courteous when answering the phone. This means using phrases such as "hello", "good morning/afternoon", "thank you" and "please" when appropriate. It also means being patient and allowing the person on the other end to speak without interruption. Being polite and courteous can help to create a positive impression and make the person on the other end of the line feel valued and respected.

Active listening is also an essential aspect of telephone manners. It's important to pay attention to what the person on the other end of the line is saying and to respond appropriately. This means asking questions and clarifying information when necessary. It also means being empathetic and understanding when the person on the other end is upset or frustrated. Active listening can help to create a positive impression and make the person on the other end feel heard and understood.

Another important aspect of telephone manners is the ability to multitask. This means being able to handle multiple calls or tasks at the same time without becoming overwhelmed or flustered. It also means being able to prioritize tasks and respond to urgent or important calls first. Being able to multitask effectively can create an impression of efficiency and competence.

Finally, it's important to be aware of the context and the purpose of the call. This means being familiar with the company's products and services, and being able to provide accurate and helpful information. It also means being aware of the person on the other end of the line, and being able to tailor the conversation to their needs and concerns. Being aware of the context and the purpose of the call can help to create a positive impression and make the person on the other end feel well-informed and well-cared for.

In conclusion, telephone manners play a crucial role in creating a positive impression and building strong relationships with customers, clients, and colleagues. They involve the use of a warm and friendly tone of voice, proper language and grammar, politeness and courteousness, active listening, multitasking and being aware of the context and purpose of the call. By practicing good telephone manners, businesses can improve their communication, create a more positive image, and ultimately increase customer satisfaction and loyalty.

It's never late to bring telephone conversation in the correct from and respectable format of speaking. Giving a positive impression over the telephone is an essential skill in any job or business, as it can greatly impact customer satisfaction and loyalty. **i want to share some tips for lasting impression in this skill.**

Use a friendly and professional tone of voice. The tone of voice is one of the most important factors in creating a positive impression over the telephone. A friendly and professional tone can indicate that you are approachable, helpful, and competent. Be sure to speak clearly and at a moderate pace, and avoid using slang or informal language.

In conclusion, giving a positive impression over the telephone is an essential skill in any job or business. It involves using a friendly and professional tone of voice, greeting the caller with a proper greeting, listening actively and showing empathy, being knowledgeable and helpful, using positive language, showing interest and building rapport, ending the call on a positive note, and following up and keeping records. By practicing these tips, you can improve your communication skills, create a more positive image, and ultimately increase customer satisfaction and loyalty.

Lets understand the importance with the help of story
Once upon a time, there was a young woman named Jane who worked as a customer service representative for a large company. Jane was known for her friendly and cheerful personality, but she had one major problem: she had a tendency to talk too much on the phone.

One day, Jane received a call from a very important customer who was calling to complain about a product they had received. Jane answered the phone with her usual enthusiasm, "Good morning! Thank you for calling XYZ company, this is Jane speaking, how can I assist you today?"

The customer, who was in a bad mood, responded curtly, "I received a defective product, and I want it fixed immediately."

Jane, not wanting to lose the customer, started talking quickly, trying to explain the company's return policy and the steps that the customer needed to take to get the product fixed. She went on and on, talking about the company's history, the quality of their products, and even the weather.

The customer, who was becoming more and more frustrated, interrupted her, "I don't need a history lesson, I just want my product fixed! Can you please just tell me what I need to do?"

Jane, realizing her mistake, apologized and quickly provided the customer with the necessary information. She even offered to expedite the process and send a replacement product right away.

The customer, impressed by Jane's willingness to help, thanked her and hung up the phone.

From that day on, Jane made a conscious effort to be more mindful of her talking on the phone. She learned to listen actively, to be brief and to the point and to always think about the customer's needs first.

As a result, her customer satisfaction ratings improved, and she was even promoted to a team lead position. She became known as the "telephone manners expert" and was often sought out by her colleagues for advice on how to handle difficult customers.

The moral of the story is that it's important to be mindful of one's talking on the phone. It's important to listen actively, to be brief and to the point, and to always think about the customer's needs first. By doing so, you can create a positive impression and build strong relationships with customers, clients and colleagues.

In conclusion, this story highlights the importance of being aware of one's telephone manners. It shows that by being mindful of how much we talk, being brief and to the point, and putting the customer's needs first, we can create a positive impression and build strong relationships. Therefore, it's important for individuals and organizations to actively encourage and promote good telephone manners in the workplace.

… BEFORE STARTING BUSINESS & JOB

CHAPTER 8

Wearing a Smile

Smiling is important because it can have a positive impact on both the person smiling and those around them. A smile can indicate friendliness and approachability, and can help to put others at ease. It can also make the person smiling feel happier and more positive. Additionally, smiling can have physical benefits such as reducing stress and lower blood pressure.

It might feel unusual to wear a smile but actually it is not every day we change the office dress and go for the work in same way a smile on the face which brings positivity and creates unimaginery aura surrounding us.

he absence of a smile in business can have a significant impact on both the individual and the organization as a whole. In customer-facing roles, a lack of smiling can make employees appear unapproachable and unfriendly, which can lead to poor customer service and ultimately harm the reputation of the business. It can also make it more difficult for employees to build relationships with customers and clients, which can negatively impact sales and business growth.

In addition to the impact on customer service and relationships, the absence of a smile can also affect employee morale and productivity. A lack of smiling can create a negative and tense work environment, which can lead to increased stress and burnout among employees. This, in turn, can lead to increased absenteeism and turnover, which can be costly for the organization.

Furthermore, in a business setting, a smile can also be a sign of professionalism and confidence. People who smile are perceived as more confident, trustworthy, and competent. On the other hand, people who don't smile may be perceived as unapproachable, unfriendly, or even unprofessional. This can affect the perception of the business and the way it is perceived by clients, customers, and other stakeholders.

Additionally, smiling is a nonverbal communication that can convey positive emotions and create positive interactions. It can help to break down barriers and build trust between people. In a business setting, this can be critical for building strong relationships with customers, clients, and colleagues.

However, it's important to note that there are some situations where a smile may not be appropriate, such as during a serious or somber meeting or during a time of grief. In these cases, it's important to be mindful of the context and to express empathy and understanding rather than a forced smile.

The absence of a smile in business can have a significant impact on both the individual and the organization as a whole. It can harm customer service and relationships, affect employee morale and productivity, and negatively impact the perception of the business. Therefore, it is important for individuals and organizations to actively encourage and promote smiling in the workplace.

Achieving The Favours With Single Formula That Is Jokes + Smiles = Successful Favour

Jokes and smiling are both important tools for building positive relationships, improving communication, and creating a more enjoyable and relaxed work environment.

When it comes to building relationships, a well-timed joke can help to break the ice and make people feel more comfortable with each other.

Joking around can also create a sense of camaraderie and inclusivity that helps to build trust and understanding between people. This is particularly important in a business setting, where building strong relationships with customers, clients, and colleagues is essential for success.

In terms of communication, jokes can be a powerful tool for getting a message across. They can make complex or difficult concepts more approachable and relatable. They can also help to diffuse tense or difficult situations by lightening the mood. This can make it easier for people to have difficult conversations or to give and receive feedback.

The act of smiling itself also plays a key role in communication. A smile can indicate friendliness and approachability, and can help to put others at ease. It can also convey positive emotions and create positive interactions. This is important in a business setting where building trust and understanding with clients, customers and colleagues is critical.

In addition to their impact on relationships and communication, jokes and smiling can also have a positive impact on employee morale and productivity. A workplace that is full of laughter and smiling is often perceived as more enjoyable and fulfilling. This can lead to increased employee satisfaction and engagement, which in turn can lead to better performance and increased productivity.

Moreover, joking and smiling can also help to reduce stress and promote mental well-being. Laughing has been shown to release endorphins, which are chemicals in the brain that can improve mood and reduce stress. Smiling also has similar effects, it can activate the release of endorphins and lower the levels of the stress hormone cortisol. This can help employees to feel more positive and energized, which can have a positive impact on their overall well-being.

However, it's important to note that not all jokes are appropriate or well-received in a business setting. It's important to be mindful of the audience and the context and to avoid jokes that could be offensive or hurtful. It's also important to make sure that the tone and delivery of the joke are appropriate and that it's not at someone else's expense.

In conclusion, jokes and smiling are important tools for building positive relationships, improving communication, and creating a more enjoyable and relaxed work environment. They can help to break the ice, build trust and understanding, improve employee morale and productivity, and promote mental well-being. Therefore, it's important for individuals and organizations to actively encourage and promote the use of jokes and smiling in the workplace.

Smile is a very powerful tool in life not less than nuclear bomb , it is a nuclear smile bomb which prosper not only your job or business but surroundings near you as well and opens the doors of success for you.

A Small Story About It Can Tell You A Lot To Remember A Lesson

Once upon a time, in a small village, there lived a boy named Jack. Jack was known for his constant frown and grumpiness. He would never smile and would always seem to be in a bad mood. The villagers avoided him, thinking that he was rude and unapproachable.

One day, an old wise man came to the village. He saw Jack sitting alone, with his usual frown on his face. The wise man approached him and asked, "Why are you always frowning, my boy? Is everything okay?"

Jack replied, "I have nothing to smile about. My life is full of hardships and I have nothing to be happy about."

The wise man smiled and said, "My dear boy, you

have everything to smile about. You have a roof over your head, food to eat, and people who care about you. Smiling is not about being happy all the time, it's about being grateful for what you have and choosing to see the positive in life."

Jack thought about the wise man's words and decided to give it a try. He started to smile, even when he didn't feel like it. And to his surprise, he started to notice the beauty of the village and the kindness of the people around him. He realized that by smiling, he was able to see the good in life.

The villagers, who had avoided Jack before, started to approach him and talk to him. They saw the change in him and started to smile back at him. Jack's smile was contagious, and soon the whole village was smiling.

Jack's life changed for the better. He became more positive and grateful for what he had. He was no longer alone and was able to build strong relationships with the people in the village. He was able to find happiness and fulfillment in the small things in life.

From that day on, Jack was known as the boy with the beautiful smile. And the villagers were forever grateful to the wise man who taught them the power of a smile.

The moral of the story is that a smile can change everything. It can change the way we see the world and the way the world sees us. It can improve our relationships and make us happier and more positive. It's important to be grateful for what we have and to choose to see the good in life, even in difficult times.

Always remember a smile is a powerful tool that can have a positive impact on our lives and the lives of those around us. It's important to practice gratitude and positivity, and to make an effort to smile, even when we don't feel like it. By doing so, we can change our perspectives, improve our relationships and find happiness in life.

CHAPTER 9

Email & Text Writing

Poor email and text writing can have a significant negative impact on business and job performance. In today's fast-paced, digital world, effective communication is crucial for success in both personal and professional settings. However, many people struggle to communicate clearly and concisely in writing, leading to confusion, misunderstandings, and wasted time and resources.

One major issue with bad email and text writing is that it can make it difficult to convey important information. When messages are poorly written, they can be hard to understand, leading to confusion and misinterpretation. This can lead to mistakes, missed deadlines, and other problems that can have serious consequences for businesses and individuals. Additionally, when messages are not clear, recipients may have to spend extra time trying to decipher their meaning, which can be frustrating and lead to a lack of trust and respect.

Another issue with bad email and text writing is that it can create a negative impression of the writer. When messages are poorly written, they can come across as unprofessional, which can harm the writer's reputation and credibility. This can be especially problematic for individuals in professional settings, where the ability to communicate effectively is critical for success. Additionally, when messages are not written well, they can be perceived as lazy or unimportant, which can lead to a lack of engagement from recipients.

Moreover, bad email and text writing can also impact our productivity, it can slow down the process of communication, leading to delays and missed deadlines. When messages are not written well, it takes longer for recipients to understand and respond to them, which can lead to delays in completing tasks and projects. This can be especially problematic in fast-paced business environments where time is of the essence.

Lastly, bad email and text writing can also lead to misunderstandings and conflicts. When messages are not written clearly, they can be misinterpreted, which can lead to misunderstandings and conflicts. This can be especially problematic in professional settings, where misunderstandings can lead to serious problems such as loss of business, damaged relationships, and legal issues.

In conclusion, bad email and text writing can have a significant negative impact on business and job performance. It can make it difficult to convey important information, create a negative impression of the writer, slow down communication process, and lead to misunderstandings and conflicts. To avoid these issues, it is important to take the time to write clear, concise, and professional messages. This can be done by using proper grammar, punctuation, and formatting, as well as by taking the time to proofread and edit messages before sending them. Additionally, it is important to be mindful of the tone and language used in messages, as these can greatly influence how they are received.

Stratergies for Writing Emails & Texts for effective communication:-

Effective email and text writing is crucial for success in today's fast-paced, digital world. Clear, concise, and professional communication can help to avoid confusion, misunderstandings, and wasted time and resources. Here are several strategies for writing effective emails and texts:

So a, clear, concise, and professional email and text writing is crucial for success in today's fast-paced, digital world. By following these strategies, you can avoid confusion, misunderstandings, and wasted time and resources. Additionally, you'll be able to create a positive impression, build trust, and increase the chances of a response. Remember, effective communication is a skill that can be learned, and the more you practice, the better you will become.

A small story will make you feel more conscious about it so let's begin.

There once was a young professional named Sarah, who had just landed her dream job as a marketing coordinator at a well-known advertising agency. She was excited to prove herself and make a positive impact on the company. However, her excitement quickly turned to frustration when she realized that her colleagues and superiors frequently had trouble understanding her emails and texts.

Sarah was known for using a lot of slang, emoji's, and informal language in her messages, thinking it would make her come across as relatable and friendly. However, this approach had the opposite effect. Her messages often seemed unprofessional, and her colleagues had trouble understanding what she was trying to say. This caused confusion and delays in completing tasks, which ultimately led to missed deadlines and lost business for the agency.

Sarah's supervisor, John, was growing increasingly frustrated with her communication style, and he had begun to lose confidence in her ability to effectively represent the company. He had even received complaints from clients about her communication, which further damaged her reputation. Despite Sarah's good intentions, her lack of professionalism in her emails and text was causing real harm to the agency's reputation and bottom line.

JOHNY EINSTEIN

John had a meeting with Sarah to discuss her communication style and provide feedback on how to improve it. He explained that using proper grammar, punctuation, and formatting, as well as avoiding slang, emoji's, and informal language, would make her messages more professional and credible. He also suggested that she take the time to proofread and edit her messages before sending them, and to be mindful of her tone and language.

Sarah took John's feedback to heart and worked hard to improve her communication skills. She made a point to use proper grammar and formatting in her messages, and to avoid using slang or emoji's. She also proofread and edited her messages before sending them, and paid close attention to her tone and language.

Through her hard work and dedication, Sarah was able to turn things around. Her colleagues and superiors began to understand her messages more easily, and she was able to complete tasks and projects on time. Her improved communication skills also helped her to build stronger relationships with clients, which led to new business for the agency.

However, despite her improvement, the damage had been done. The lost clients and missed deadlines had cost the agency a significant amount of money, and Sarah's supervisor John had to let her go. Sarah was devastated, she realized that her lack of attention to her email and text writing had cost her not only her job, but also a valuable opportunity to prove herself and advance her career.

This story serves as a reminder of the importance of effective email and text writing. Clear, concise, and professional communication is crucial for success in both personal and professional settings. Poor communication can lead to confusion, misunderstandings, and wasted time and resources, and can even cost people their jobs and businesses. It's important to take the time to write clear, concise, and professional messages, and to be mindful of the tone and language used in messages, as these can greatly influence how they are received.

CHAPTER-10

Respect Every Opinion & Gender

To understand this theme of topic one need to understand "What is Opinion?"

An opinion is a view or judgment formed about something, not necessarily based on fact or knowledge. It is a personal perspective or belief that someone holds on a particular subject. Opinions can be positive, negative, or neutral and can vary widely among different people. They are subjective in nature and can be influenced by a person's personal experiences, values, and beliefs.

Opinions can be expressed in various forms such as in written, verbal or nonverbal forms. They can also be expressed by an individual or a group of people. Opinions can be based on facts or on personal beliefs, it can be supported by evidence or it can be formed without any supporting evidence.

Opinions can also be useful in decision-making, as they provide a different perspective on a subject and can help to broaden understanding. However, it is important to remember that opinions are not facts and should be considered alongside other information and evidence before making a decision.

Is it necessary to listen every opinion? Undoubtedly the answer is yes but why not no that's a thinkable question. If we dive deeper into it the answer is

Listening to every opinion is important for a number of reasons:

It's important to note that while it's necessary to listen every opinion, it's also important to evaluate them in the light of facts and evidence. Everyone has the right to express their opinion, but it's also important to consider the reasoning and evidence behind them. It's also important to respect the opinion of others, but it doesn't mean that you have to agree with them. Listening to every opinion and giving them the proper consideration can lead to more informed decisions, better problem-solving and a more inclusive and respectful environment.

What Happen If Don't Listen And Understand Opinion In The Business Or In Job?

If opinions are not listened to and understood in a business or job setting, it can lead to a number of negative consequences:

In conclusion, listening and understanding opinions is

crucial in a business or job setting. It allows for diversity of thought, promotes inclusivity and respect, improves communication, and leads to better decision-making. When opinions are not heard and understood, it can lead to a number of negative consequences, such as decreased productivity, increased conflict, damaged relationships, and poor decision-making, which can ultimately harm the company's performance.

I understand it's easy to say but difficult to bring into habit There are many ways through which you can improve your opinion skills and they are so easy just follows these guidelines in your daily life

Here are some ways to improve your opinion skills:

It's important to note that improving your opinion skills takes time and practice, but it's worth the effort. With improved opinion skills, you'll be able to communicate more effectively, collaborate more effectively, and make better decisions. Additionally, you'll be able to build stronger relationships and contribute to a more inclusive and respectful work environment.

Golden way to practice is just open a conversation cum debate with your partner particularly on topics where you carry different opinions and listen to them accept them but the topic should be of mutual agreement before the beginning of discussion so it may not affect your relationship

Gender :- Gender refers to the socially constructed roles, behaviors, and identities that a society considers appropriate for men and women. It is distinct from biological sex, which refers to the physical and physiological characteristics that define males and females.

The concept of gender is complex and multifaceted, and it can vary greatly across different cultures and historical periods. In many societies, gender roles and expectations are rigidly defined, with little room for deviation or individuality. For example, in some cultures, men are expected to be strong and assertive, while women are expected to be nurturing and submissive.

Gender identity, on the other hand, refers to an individual's internal sense of their own gender, which may or may not align with the sex they were assigned at birth. This can include cisgender individuals, whose gender identity aligns with their assigned sex, as well as transgender individuals, whose gender identity does not align with their assigned sex.

Discrimination around gender have existed for centuries, but in recent years, there has been a growing movement to recognize and celebrate gender diversity. This includes the recognition of non-binary gender identities, which fall outside of the traditional binary of male and female. Many people are now identifying as genderqueer, non-binary, or gender non-conforming, which means they do not identify exclusively as male or female.

It is important to note that gender roles, identities, and expectations can have a significant impact on an individual's mental and physical well-being. Individuals who do not conform to societal expectations of gender may face discrimination, marginalization, and even violence. On the other hand, individuals who are able to express their gender identity authentically and without fear of discrimination may experience greater well-being and happiness.

Why gender equality is important in job & business ?

Gender equality is important in the workplace and in business for a variety of reasons.

Firstly, it is a basic human right for all individuals to have equal opportunities and treatment regardless of their gender. Gender inequality in the workplace can lead to discrimination, marginalization, and a lack of representation for certain groups of people. This can have a negative impact on both the individuals affected and the overall success of the business.

Secondly, gender equality leads to a more diverse and inclusive workforce. Research has shown that companies with more diverse teams tend to have better financial performance, greater innovation, and improved decision-making. A more diverse workforce also leads to a better understanding and representation of the customer base.

Thirdly, promoting gender equality in the workplace can help to attract and retain top talent. Companies that are seen as inclusive and fair are more likely to attract and retain the best employees, regardless of their gender. A fair and inclusive workplace also leads to increased employee satisfaction, engagement and productivity.

Lastly, gender equality is a business and economic imperative. Women constitute half of the global population and their full participation in the labor force is essential for economic growth, development and stability.

It's important to note that improving gender equality is an ongoing process, and requires commitment and sustained effort from management, employees, and other stakeholders. It's also important to remember that it's not just about hiring and promoting more women, it's also about creating a culture and policies that allow them to thrive and succeed.

There are several ways to improve gender equality in the workplace and in business:

CHAPTER-11

Morale

What is Morale?
Morale is the emotional and mental state of an individual or group of individuals, with regard to their attitude towards their work or task and their sense of personal well-being.

Why Morale Is Important In Job And Business ?

Morale is important in the workplace and in business for a variety of reasons:

morale is important in the workplace and in business because it can lead to increased productivity, improved employee retention, better customer service, reduced absenteeism, a positive impact on the bottom line, and a positive company culture. A high morale can benefit both employees and the organization as a whole.

Why Person Without Morale Is Not Respected In The Business Or In A Job?

A person without morale is not respected because they are perceived as lacking in certain positive qualities or characteristics.

It's important to note that a person's morale can change over time, and a person who is perceived as lacking in morale may be able to improve their situation by working on the above mentioned areas. Additionally, a person's morale can be affected by many factors, including personal life, economic or political situation, or even the global events that can create a sense of uncertainty or fear.

Once upon a time, in a small village, there lived a farmer named Jack. Jack was a hard-working man, but he had always struggled with low morale. He felt unappreciated and unimportant, and it showed in the way he approached his work. He was often grumpy and complained about his lot in life.

One day, a wise old sage came to the village. He observed Jack's farm and noticed how unkempt it was, and how little care Jack took in his work. The sage approached Jack and asked him why he seemed so unhappy. Jack explained his feelings of inadequacy and his belief that no one appreciated his work.

The sage smiled and told Jack a story. He spoke of a farmer who, like Jack, had always struggled with low morale. But one day, he decided to change his attitude. He began to approach his work with a sense of purpose and pride. He took extra care to tend to his crops and animals, and he began to see the beauty in the hard work he did.

As time passed, the farmer's crops flourished, and his animals grew healthy and strong. His neighbors began to notice the change in him and the positive impact it had on his farm. They began to respect and admire him for his hard work and dedication.

Jack listened carefully to the sage's story and realized that he too could change his attitude and improve his morale. He decided to take pride in his work, and to approach it with a sense of purpose and dedication. He began to tend to his farm with care and saw his crops flourish, and his animals grow healthy.

His neighbors, who had once ignored him, now began to respect and admire him for his hard work and dedication. Jack was no longer grumpy and complaining, he was happy and fulfilled, and his morale had greatly improved.

The moral of the story is that our attitude and morale can greatly impact our work and how we are perceived by others. With a positive attitude and high morale, we can achieve great things and earn the respect and admiration of those around us.

AFTERWORD

I am thankful for the people who supported me , this book is all about personal experience which i want to share with you all in the human society even without college degree if you own these qualities success is all your in every venture of your life.

www.ingramcontent.com/pod-product-compliance
Lightning Source LLC
Chambersburg PA
CBHW071148240526
45465CB00024BA/1887